D1532557

Ankylosaurus

Kimberley Jane Pryor

mc Marshall Cavendish Benchmark
New York

This edition first published in 2012 in the United States of America by Marshall Cavendish Benchmark
An imprint of Marshall Cavendish Corporation

Website: www.marshallcavendish.us

This publication represents the opinions and views of the author based on Kimberley Jane Pryor's personal experience, knowledge, and research. The information in this book serves as a general guide only. The author and publisher have used their best efforts in preparing this book and disclaim liability rising directly and indirectly from the use and application of this book.

Other Marshall Cavendish Offices:
Marshall Cavendish International (Asia) Private Limited, 1 New Industrial Road, Singapore 536196 • Marshall Cavendish International (Thailand) Co Ltd. 253 Asoke, 12th Flr, Sukhumvit 21 Road, Klongtoey Nua, Wattana, Bangkok 10110, Thailand • Marshall Cavendish (Malaysia) Sdn Bhd, Times Subang, Lot 46, Subang Hi-Tech Industrial Park, Batu Tiga, 40000 Shah Alam, Selangor Darul Ehsan, Malaysia

Marshall Cavendish is a trademark of Times Publishing Limited

Library of Congress Cataloging-in-Publication Data

Pryor, Kimberley Jane.
   Ankylosaurus / Kimberley Jane Pryor.
      p. cm. — (Discovering Dinosaurs)
   Summary: "Discusses the physical characteristics, time period, diet, and habitat of the Ankylosaurus" —Provided by publisher.
   Includes bibliographical references and index.
   ISBN 978-1-60870-535-1
   1. Ankylosaurus—Juvenile literature. I. Title.
   QE862.O65P79 2012
   567.915—dc22
                        2010037185

First published in 2011 by
MACMILLAN EDUCATION AUSTRALIA PTY LTD
15–19 Claremont Street, South Yarra 3141

Visit our website at www.macmillan.com.au or go directly to www.macmillanlibrary.com.au

Associated companies and representatives throughout the world.

Copyright text © Kimberley Jane Pryor 2011

Publisher: Carmel Heron
Commissioning Editor: Niki Horin
Managing Editor: Vanessa Lanaway
Editor: Laura Jeanne Gobal
Proofreader: Helena Newton
Designer: Kerri Wilson (cover and text)
Page Layout: Pier Vido and Domenic Lauricella
Photo Researcher: Brendan Gallagher
Illustrator: Melissa Webb
Production Controller: Vanessa Johnson

Printed in China

Acknowledgments
The author and publisher are grateful to the following for permission to reproduce copyright material:

Photographs courtesy of: John Rodriguez, 29; Photolibrary/ James L. Amos, 9; Royal Tyrrell Museum, Drumheller, Alberta, Canada, 8; WitmerLab at Ohio University, 14.

Background image of ripples on water © Shutterstock/ArchMan.

While every care has been taken to trace and acknowledge copyright, the publisher tenders their apologies for any accidental infringement where copyright has proved untraceable. They would be pleased to come to a suitable arrangement with the rightful owner in each case.

For Nick, Thomas, and Ashley

1 3 5 6 4 2

Contents

When a word is printed in **bold**, you can look up its meaning in the glossary on page 31.

What Are Dinosaurs?

Dinosaurs (*dy-no-soars*) were **reptiles** that lived millions of years ago. They were different from other reptiles because their legs were directly under their bodies instead of to their sides like today's reptiles. Dinosaurs walked or ran on land.

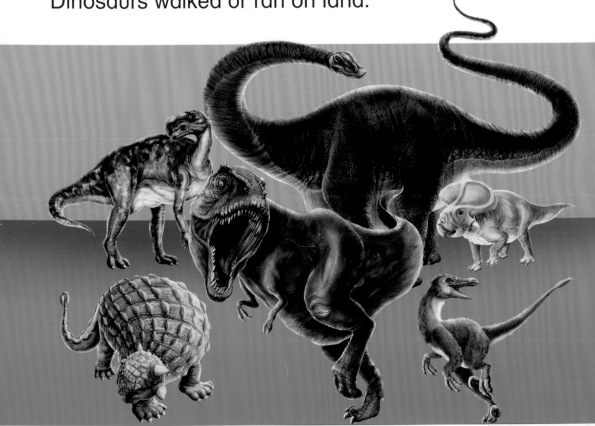

At one time, there were more than 1,000 different kinds of dinosaurs

Dinosaurs lived during a period of time called the Mesozoic (*mes-ah-zoh-ik*) Era. The Mesozoic Era is divided into the Triassic (*try-ass-ik*), Jurassic (*je-rass-ik*), and Cretaceous (*krah-tay-shahs*) periods.

This timeline shows the three different periods of the Mesozoic Era, when dinosaurs lived.

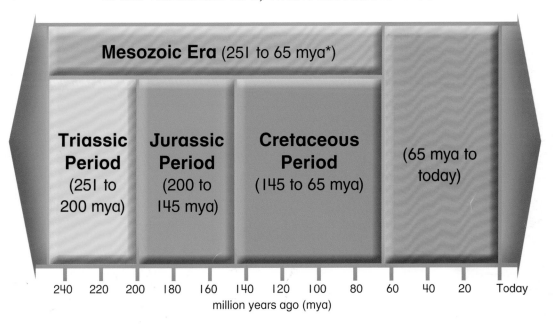

*Note: mya = million years ago

Dinosaur Groups

Dinosaurs are sorted into two main groups according to their hipbones. Some dinosaurs had hipbones like a lizard's. Other dinosaurs had hipbones like a bird's.

All dinosaurs were either lizard-hipped or bird-hipped.

Dinosaurs

Lizard-hipped dinosaurs

Bird-hipped dinosaurs

Dinosaurs can be sorted into five smaller groups. Some lizard-hipped dinosaurs walked on two legs and ate meat. Others walked on four legs and ate plants. All bird-hipped dinosaurs ate plants.

Main Group	Smaller Group	Features	Examples
Lizard-hipped	Theropoda (*ther-ah-poh-dah*)	• Small to large • Walked on two legs • Meat-eaters	Tyrannosaurus Velociraptor
	Sauropodomorpha (*soar-rop-ah-dah-mor-fah*)	• Huge • Walked on four legs • Plant-eaters	Diplodocus
	Thyreophora (*theer-ee-off-or-ah*)	• Small to large • Walked on four legs • Plant-eaters	Ankylosaurus
Bird-hipped	Ornithopoda (*or-ni-thop-oh-dah*)	• Small to large • Walked on two or four legs • Plant-eaters	Muttaburrasaurus
	Ceratopsia (*ser-ah-top-see-ah*)	• Small to large • Walked on two or four legs • Plant-eaters • Frilled and horned skulls	Protoceratops

This table shows how dinosaurs can be sorted according to their size, how they walked, and the food they ate.

How Do We Know about Dinosaurs?

We know about dinosaurs because people have found fossils. Fossils are the preserved remains of plants and animals that lived long ago. They include bones, teeth, footprints, and eggs.

This fossil is the tail club of an Ankylosaurus.

People who study fossils are called paleontologists (*pail-ee-on-tol-oh-jists*). They study fossils to learn about dinosaurs. They also remove dinosaur bones from rocks and rebuild **skeletons**.

dinosaur bones

Paleontologists carefully chip away the rock to uncover dinosaur bones.

Meet Ankylosaurus

Ankylosaurus (*an-ky-loh-soar-us*) was a large, bird-hipped dinosaur. It belonged to a group of dinosaurs called thyreophora. Dinosaurs in this group walked on four legs and ate plants.

Ankylosaurus had an armor made of bony plates and spikes that covered its body.

Ankylosaurus lived in the late Cretaceous period, between 70 and 65 million years ago.

The purple area on this timeline shows when Ankylosaurus lived.

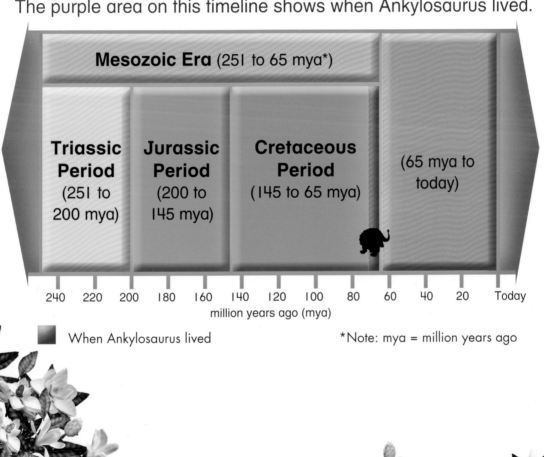

Mesozoic Era (251 to 65 mya*)

Triassic Period (251 to 200 mya)

Jurassic Period (200 to 145 mya)

Cretaceous Period (145 to 65 mya)

(65 mya to today)

240 220 200 180 160 140 120 100 80 60 40 20 Today

million years ago (mya)

When Ankylosaurus lived

*Note: mya = million years ago

What Did Ankylosaurus Look Like?

Ankylosaurus was 33 feet (10 meters) long and 10 feet (3 meters) tall at the hips. It weighed about 5 tons (4.5 tonnes).

Ankylosaurus was as big as an army tank and heavier than a rhinoceros!

bony tail club

bony plates

Ankylosaurus walked on four legs. It had a wide head with a beak and horns. Ankylosaurus had a large, bony tail club, and **armor** made of bony plates and spikes.

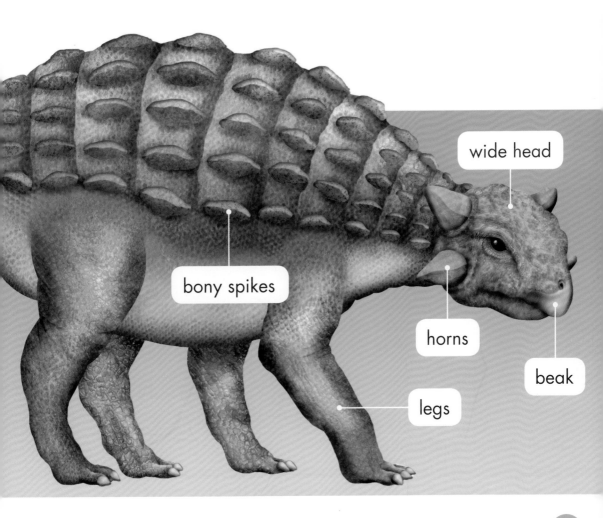

wide head

bony spikes

horns

beak

legs

The Skull and Senses of Ankylosaurus

Ankylosaurus had a wide and very thick skull. There was room for only a tiny brain. This means that Ankylosaurus was not smart! When seen from above, its skull looks triangle-shaped.

wide, thick skull

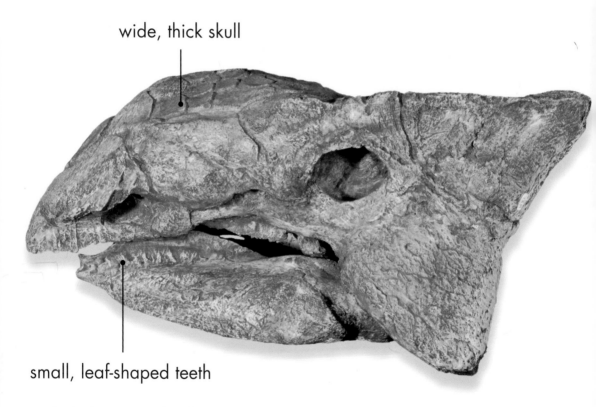

small, leaf-shaped teeth

Ankylosaurus had small, leaf-shaped teeth.

Ankylosaurus could see its surroundings quite well. This is because its eyes were on the sides of its head. Passages in its nose may have strengthened its **sense** of smell.

The Senses of Ankylosaurus				
Sense	Very Good	Good	Fair	Unable to Say
Sight			✔	
Hearing			✔	
Smell		✔		
Taste				✔
Touch				✔

Ankylosaurus Fossils

Ankylosaurus fossils have been found in the United States and Canada.

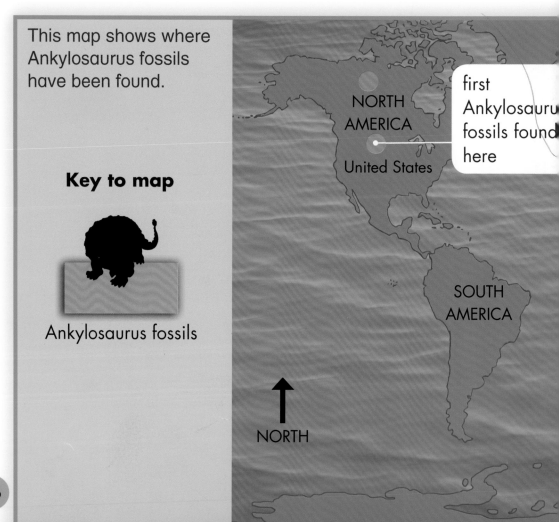

This map shows where Ankylosaurus fossils have been found.

Key to map

Ankylosaurus fossils

NORTH AMERICA

United States

first Ankylosauru fossils found here

SOUTH AMERICA

NORTH

In 1906, paleontologist Barnum Brown found the first Ankylosaurus fossils. He found bones, armor, and part of a skull in Montana.

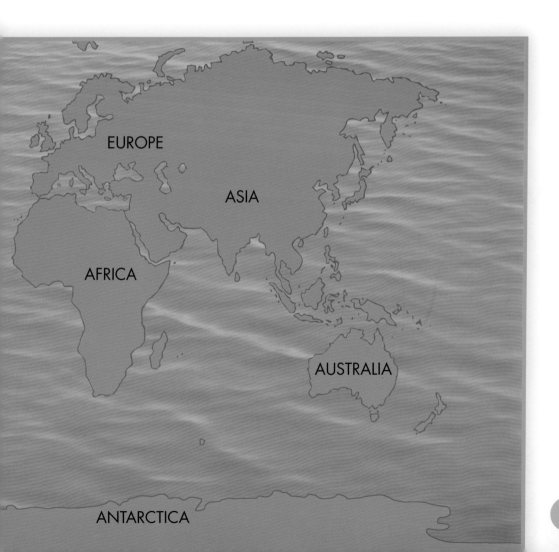

EUROPE

ASIA

AFRICA

AUSTRALIA

ANTARCTICA

Where Did Ankylosaurus Live?

Ankylosaurus lived on a coastal **plain** that was mostly covered with small trees. The plain was near a shallow sea that once separated western and eastern North America.

lichens

moss

The first flowering plants, such as magnolias,
appeared on the coastal plain. Moss and **lichens**
also grew there.

Ankylosaurus could live in the open because its
armor protected it from predators.

coastal plain

magnolias

What Did Ankylosaurus Eat?

Ankylosaurus was a herbivore, or plant-eater. It ate soft plants that grew on or near the ground. It ate these because it was not tall enough to reach plants that were higher up.

Foods Eaten by Ankylosaurus	
Leaves	
Lichens	
Moss	
Twigs	

Paleontologists think Ankylosaurus ate most kinds of plants within its reach. This is because the wide beak of the Ankylosaurus was strong enough to gather many kinds of plants.

Ankylosaurus used its wide beak to nip leaves off branches.

Predator or Prey?

It is thought that Ankylosaurus was **prey** for large, meat-eating dinosaurs. However, Ankylosaurus would not have been easily caught because of its armor and tail club.

Ankylosaurus may have been hunted by Tyrannosaurus (*ty-ran-oh-soar-us*), but would not have been easily caught.

Ankylosaurus was protected by its armor. It could have swung its tail club at **predators**. The tail club of Ankylosaurus was so heavy and large that it could break bones.

An adult Ankylosaurus could have used its tail club to smash the knee of a Tyrannosaurus.

How Did Ankylosaurus Live?

Some paleontologists think Ankylosaurus lived in a herd, or group. This is because other dinosaurs similar to Ankylosaurus lived in herds. However, there is no proof that Ankylosaurus did.

Ankylosaurus was so heavily armored that it would have been safe living alone.

Ankylosaurus spent most of its time eating. It had to eat a lot of food to supply its heavy body with **energy**.

Ankylosaurus was such a large dinosaur that it spent almost all day eating.

Life Cycle of Ankylosaurus

Paleontologists study fossils and living animals to learn about the life cycle of Ankylosaurus.

1. An adult male Ankylosaurus displayed his tail club to attract a female. The male and female **mated**.

4. The baby Ankylosauruses stayed with their mothers until they were old enough to find food alone. They grew into adults.

They believe there were four main stages in the life cycle of Ankylosaurus. This is what it may have been like.

2. The female laid eggs in a nest on the ground. She stayed near the nest to guard the eggs from predators.

3. Baby Ankylosauruses hatched from the eggs. Their mothers brought them plants to eat.

What Happened to Ankylosaurus?

Ankylosaurus became **extinct** about 65 million years ago. Many paleontologists think it died out when a large **meteorite** hit Earth. A meteorite would have caused most plants and animals to die.

1. A large meteorite hits Earth, causing dust clouds that block out the sun.

2. Plants get no sunshine and die.

3. Dinosaurs run out of food and die.

The meteorite impact would have caused dust clouds, which would have blocked out the sun.

Some paleontologists think Ankylosaurus was dying out before the meteorite hit Earth. This is because Earth's **climate** was changing. Also, volcanoes were releasing **lava** and poisonous gases, which would have affected Ankylosaurus.

Ankylosaurus could not survive changing conditions on Earth, leaving us with only fossils.

Names and Their Meanings

Dinosaurs are named by people who discover them or paleontologists who study them. A dinosaur may be named for its appearance or behavior. Its name may also honor a person or place.

Name	Meaning
Dinosaur	Terrible lizard—because people thought dinosaurs were powerful lizards
Ankylosaurus	Fused lizard—because many of its bones were joined together
Diplodocus	Double beam—because it had special bones in its tail
Muttaburrasaurus	Muttaburra lizard—because it was discovered near the town of Muttaburra, in Australia
Protoceratops	First horned face—because it was one of the early horned dinosaurs
Tyrannosaurus	Tyrant lizard—because it was a fearsome ruler of the land
Velociraptor	Speedy thief—because it ran quickly and ate meat

Glossary

armor	A strong, protective covering for the body
climate	The usual weather in a place.
energy	The power that allows people and animals to be active.
extinct	No longer existing.
lava	The very hot, melted rock that flows out of a volcano.
lichens	Fungi growing together with plants called algae.
mated	Created offspring.
meteorite	A rock from space that has landed on Earth.
plain	A wide, flat area of land.
predators	Animals that hunt and kill other animals for food.
prey	An animal that is hunted and killed by other animals for food.
reptiles	Creeping or crawling animals that are covered with scales.
sense	A special ability that people and animals use to experience the world around them. Typically, those senses are sight, hearing, smell, taste, and touch.
skeletons	The bones inside the body of a person or an animal.

Index